for Jean

Arrival of the Queen of

(from 'Solomon')

Arranged by
WATSON FORBES

G. F. HANDEL

When the duet string versions are performed, the pianist should play the notes in small type and omit the sections in brackets.
Duration: 3 minutes

© Oxford University Press 1963
Printed in Great Britain
OXFORD UNIVERSITY PRESS, MUSIC DEPARTMENT, GREAT CLARENDON STREET, OXFORD OX2 6DP
Photocopying this copyright material is ILLEGAL.

f
f
f
f
cresc.
cresc.
B
f
p
f
p
C
mf
p
mf
staccato
p

cresc.
mf
cresc.
mf staccato
D
f
f
p
p
cresc.
cresc.
mf
p
mf
p
E

cresc. poco a poco
cresc. poco a poco
non legato
F
f
p
mf
f
p
mf staccato
G
p
p
cresc.
mf
cresc.
mf

for Jean

Arrival of the Queen of Sheba

(from 'Solomon')

Arranged for Violin and Piano by
WATSON FORBES

G. F. HANDEL

Violin

Allegro (♩ = 120)

f *simile* *f*

f

A

mf *cresc.*

f *f*

cresc. *f*

B

p *mf*

C

p *cresc.*

mf D *f*

p

cresc. *mf* *p* E

cresc. poco a poco

© Oxford University Press 1963

Printed in Great Britain
OXFORD UNIVERSITY PRESS, MUSIC DEPARTMENT, GREAT CLARENDON STREET, OXFORD OX2 6DP

Photocopying this copyright material is ILLEGAL.

F
f
p
mf
G
p
cresc.
H
mf
f
mf
cresc.
f
tr
J
p leggiero
cresc.
K
mf
p
cresc. poco a poco
L
f
mp
mp
cresc.
M
mf
cresc.
f
N
f
f allarg.
tr

for Jean

Arrival of the Queen of Sheba

(from 'Solomon')

Arranged for two Violins and Piano by
WATSON FORBES

G. F. HANDEL

2nd Violin

© Oxford University Press 1963

Printed in Great Britain
OXFORD UNIVERSITY PRESS, MUSIC DEPARTMENT, GREAT CLARENDON STREET, OXFORD OX2 6DP

Photocopying this copyright material is ILLEGAL.

G
mf
p
cresc.
mf
H
f
mf
p
cresc.
f
J
p leggiero
cresc.
K
mf
p
cresc. poco a poco
L
f
p
mp
cresc.
M
mf
cresc.
f
N
f
f allarg.

for Jean

Arrival of the Queen of Sheba

(from 'Solomon')

Arranged for two Violas and Piano
(or Violin, Viola and Piano) by
WATSON FORBES

G. F. HANDEL

2nd Viola

© Oxford University Press 1963

Printed in Great Britain
OXFORD UNIVERSITY PRESS, MUSIC DEPARTMENT, GREAT CLARENDON STREET, OXFORD OX2 6DP

Photocopying this copyright material is ILLEGAL.

G
mf
p
cresc.
mf
H
f
mf
p
cresc.
f
J
p leggiero
cresc.
K
mf
p
cresc. poco a poco
L
f
p
mp
cresc.
M
mf
cresc.
f
N
f
f allarg.

for Jean

Arrival of the Queen of Sheba

(from 'Solomon')

Arranged for Viola and Piano by
WATSON FORBES

G. F. HANDEL

Viola

© Oxford University Press 1963

Printed in Great Britain
OXFORD UNIVERSITY PRESS, MUSIC DEPARTMENT, GREAT CLARENDON STREET, OXFORD OX2 6DP

Photocopying this copyright material is ILLEGAL.

F
f
p
mf
G
p
cresc.
H
mf
f
mf
cresc.
tr
f
tr
J
p leggiero
cresc.
K
mf
p
cresc. poco a poco
L
f
mp
mp cresc.
M
mf
cresc.
f
N
f
f allarg.
tr

H
f
mf
non legato
dim.
mf
cresc.
tr
p
cresc.
f
tr
J
p leggiero
f
pp staccato
cresc.
K
mf
cresc.
mf

p
cresc. poco a poco
p staccato
cresc. poco a poco
L
f
f
mp
p

Processed and printed by
Halstan & Co. Ltd., Amersham, Bucks., England

OXFORD UNIVERSITY PRESS